PRAYING TOGETHER
in word and song

second revised edition

Taizé

MOWBRAY

CONTENTS

Meditative singing *page* 4

Verses from the Psalms 5

Bible readings 13

Silence 19

Intercessions: prayer for all humanity 20

Prayers by Brother Roger 27

A Prayer around the Cross 36

Can some of these ideas be used for our Sunday morning worship? 38

Arranging the church or room for prayer 38

Songs and Chants 39

INDEX TO SONGS AND CHANTS

no.

1 Alleluia 2 *Page* 40

2 Alleluia 4 40

3 Alleluia 7 40

4 Kyrie 1 41

5 Kyrie 6 41

6 Kyrie 10 41

7 Adoramus te Domine 42

8 Beatitudes 42

9 Benedictus 43

10 Bless the Lord 44

11 Confitemini Domino 45

12 Dona nobis pacem 46

13 Gloria 47

14 Gloria Patri 48

15 In Our Darkness *page* 49

16 Jubilate Deo 50

17 Jubilate servite 50

18 Laudate omnes gentes 51

19 Magnificat 52

20 My soul is at rest 53

21 O Lord, hear my prayer 54

22 Ostende nobis 55

23 Sanctum nomen Domini 56

24 Stay with us 57

25 Surrexit 58

26 Tallis' Canon 59

27 The Lord is my light 60

28 Ubi caritas 61

29 Veni Creator Spiritus 61

A generous common prayer

The central event in the daily life of our community, and in which all visitors take part, is common prayer, morning, midday and evening. Many people are thirsting for prayer together to be a vital part of their own Christian commitment at home, in their own local church community.

How can we pray together, yet leave each person free to "Be still and know that I am God"? How can our prayer together, by its simple beauty, be expressive of the mystery of God? How can our prayer gather people of all ages — young people, children, the older generations — and thus help us to sense the universality of our communion together? In a word, how can local church communities discover a generous common prayer? There are no ready-made answers to this question. We would only like the ideas and material in this book to be of practical encouragement.

Throughout the book, the ideas given as notes at the bottom of the pages come from suggestions made by people based on their own experiences of preparing prayer together in local churches.

Meditative singing

It is good if the prayer can begin by gathering in silence, perhaps using prayerful music (for example, classical guitar or organ music by J. S. Bach), or else with the singing of a meditative chant while people are coming in. In this way there is no abrupt break between prayer and daily life.

Repetitive chants have a certain element of spontaneity which hymns lack: they last as long as people want to sing. Some of the very simple more meditative chants (for example Confitemini, Adoramus te, Bless the Lord, etc.) can easily be sustained very quietly for several minutes even by just one or two people, until little by little other people realize that it is a prayer in which they can join too. In leading the prayer in this way there is an element of daring: to continue singing until the chant becomes a prayer for oneself, and at the same time an invitation to others to pray.

At the end of the prayer, while some gather little by little in another room to meet, others may wish to stay on to pray in silence or singing a meditative chant. They are staying to 'watch and pray with Christ' as he asked his disciples to do — a prayer limited to just a few words, but which awakens the attention of the heart.

Sometimes you will need to have a short song-practice (see page 41) before the prayer: the chants used in this book can all be picked up easily, but it will help to give those who do not know the Latin songs at least the words of each song you will be using, together with a translation of what they mean.

In order to avoid all announcements during the prayer like 'Song no. 5!' teach the music in the order in which it will be sung during the prayer. And, as you teach the music, explain very simply the form the prayer will take, for example: '. . . after the readings we shall sing "Ubi Caritas", and then there will be a long moment of silence, at the end of the silence we shall stand up and sing "Kyrie Eleison", which means "Lord have mercy", and then there will be a time when those who wish can pray for others, we can all associate ourselves to each intercession by singing "Kyrie Eleison" after each person prays. . .'.

Verses from the Psalms

When all have arrived, one or two people can read (or sing) the verses of a psalm while everyone sings an *Alleluia* (page 40) or other response after each verse.

For thousands of years the People of God have used the Psalms to express their waiting on God. Singing the same words, we are one with them. Jesus himself prayed the Psalms.

How lovely is your dwelling-place,
O Lord, God Almighty!
My soul is longing and yearning
for the courts of the Lord.
My heart and my being ring out their joy
to you, the Living God.

Even the sparrow has found a home
and the swallow a nest for her young:
by your altar, O Lord Almighty,
my King and my God.

Blessed those who dwell in your house
for ever singing your praise,
blessed those whose strength is in you
and who seek out your roads.

They pass through the valley of tears
and they make it a place of springs;
with gathering strength they walk,
in Sion they will see their God.

In addition to the Psalms given here, these others also lend themselves to use in prayer together, and particularly those in bold type: Psalm nos. 5, 8, 15, 16, **19, 23, 25,** 27, 30, 32, 33, 40, **43,** 47, 57, **62, 63,** 65, 66, 70, **71, 85,** 86, **91,** 93, **95, 96, 98, 100,** 111, **113, 116,** 118, 119, 122, 126, **138,** 143, 145, **146,** 150. When you use these Psalms for prayer, do not hesitate to select just the verses which are easily accessible.

The numbering of the Psalms used here is the Hebrew numbering, used in nearly all Bibles.

Lord God, hear my prayer,
lend an attentive ear;
turn and see, O God our shield,
look upon the face of your Christ.

One day within your courts
is better than a thousand elsewhere;
I prefer the doorway of the house of God
to the home of the ungodly.
Lord God Almighty, happy are those who trust in you!

(from Psalm 84)

I will bless the Lord at all times,
on my lips, the sound of his praise;
give glory, my soul, to the Lord,
all the humble, hear and rejoice.

Come, let us worship the Lord,
with one voice give glory to God;
I cried to the Lord, he replied,
he freed me when I was afraid.

With God is the fullness of joys,
turn to him, you will not be deceived;
when the poor cry out, he gives heed,
he is close to all in distress.

The angel of God is near,
he defends the faithful of heart;
how good is the Lord! Taste and see!
What joy when he is our guard!

In anguish, the just call on God,
he saves them from all their distress;
broken hearts are dear to the Lord,
he raises their souls from despair.

(from Ps. 34)

Bless the Lord, my soul,
all my being, bless his holy name.
Bless the Lord, my soul,
forget none of his good deeds.

It is God who forgives all your sins,
and heals your diseases;
who redeems your life from death,
who crowns you with love and compassion.
He fills your life with every kind of good,
and like an eagle, your youth is renewed.

The Lord is compassionate
and rich in merciful love.
He does not treat us as our sins deserve
nor repay us according to our faults.
For as high as the heavens are above the earth
so strong is his love for those who revere him.

As far as the east is from the west
he takes away our sins.
As tenderly as a father treats his children,
so the Lord treats who revere him.
For God knows of what we are made,
he remembers that we are dust.

Human life is like the grass,
it blooms like the flower of the field.
Then the wind blows and it is gone,
never to be seen again.
But God's love is everlasting
upon those who hold him holy;
his justice reaches out upon the generations
when they keep his covenant in truth.

The Lord has established his rule in heaven,
his kingdom is above all else.
Bless the Lord, you his angels,
you mighty ones who do his bidding
and heed the voice of his word.
Bless the Lord, O my soul!

(from Ps. 103)

O Lord, you have searched me and you know me.
You know when I sit and when I rise,
you follow my thoughts from afar.
You see my going out and my lying down:
all my ways lie open to you.

Before a word is on my lips
you know it completely, Lord.
You hem me in, behind and before;
you have laid your hand upon me.
Such knowledge is beyond me,
a height to which I cannot attain.

So where can I escape from your spirit?
Where can I flee from your presence?
If I go up to heaven, you are there,
if I lie in the tomb, you are there.

If I speed away on the wings of the dawn,
and settle on the far side of the sea,
even there your hand will guide me,
your right hand will hold me fast.

If I say, 'I will hide in the dark,
let the light around me be night,'
even darkness is not dark for you
and the night is as clear as the day.

For you created my being
and wove me in my mother's womb.
I thank you for the wonder of my being;
what wonders all your works reveal!

How precious to me are your thoughts, O God!
How many they are!
If I try to count them,
they outnumber the grains of sand;
to finish, I must be eternal, like you. *(to next page)*

Search me, O God, and know my heart,
test me and know my thoughts.
See that I do not follow a path that is wrong
and guide me onto the way that leads to eternity.

(from Ps. 139)

Like a deer that yearns
 for a cooling stream
so my soul is athirst
 for you, my God.

My soul is thirsting for God,
 for the living God;
when shall I come and behold
 the face of God?

Tears are my only food
 by night and by day;
always I hear them say:
 Where is your God?

Once I went with the throng
 to the House of our God,
with shouts of rejoicing and praise
 on the lips of the crowd.

If by day the Lord is pleased
 to reveal his love,
his song in my heart by night
 prays the God of my life.

What weighs you down, my soul?
 Why faint in my breast?
Hope in God: I will praise him still,
 my Saviour, my God.

(from Ps. 42)

Out of the depths I call to you,
Lord, hear my cry!
Let your ear be attentive to my voice.

If you, Lord, keep record of our sins,
then who could stand?
But with you there is forgiveness,
and therefore we adore you.

My soul is longing for the Lord,
I count on his word.
My Soul is waiting for the Lord
more than watchmen wait for the break of day.

Put your hope in God,
because with him is unfailing love
and fullness of redemption.
Indeed God will redeem his people
from all their sins.

(from Ps. 130)

I lift up my eyes to the hills:
where is my help to come from?
My help comes from the Lord,
who made both heaven and earth.

He will not let you stumble or fall,
your guardian will not sleep.
No, as the guardian of his people,
he never falls asleep.

The Lord is your guardian and your shade,
he stays close at hand;
the sun will not strike you by day,
nor the moon by night.

The Lord will keep you from harm
he watches over your life;
the Lord watches over you as you come and go,
both now and for evermore.

(from Ps. 121)

God is with us, our shelter and strength,
our help in distress, he is close at hand;
then how should we fear, though the earth gives way
or the mountains are hurled to the depths of the sea?

Like a stream, joy flows to the house of God,
its waters gladden his holy place;
God is there, it cannot be destroyed,
God will send help at the dawn of day.

Behold and see what the Lord has done,
the One who says:
'Be still and know that I am God;
I will be exalted among the nations
and upon the whole earth.'

(from Ps. 46)

Have mercy upon me, O God,
according to your unfailing love;
in your compassion blot out all my sin,
wash away the stain of my faults.

I will confess the wrong I have done,
I remember all my offences.
You desire sincerity of heart,
so instruct me deep within of your truth;
purify me, that I may be clean,
wash me, and I shall be whiter than snow.

Create in me, O God, a new heart,
and renew a steadfast spirit within me.
Do not cast me away from your presence,
or take your Holy Spirit from me.
Restore to me the joy of your salvation,
give me a willing spirit, to sustain me.

Save me from guilt, O God, and rescue me,
your justice shall become my song;
O Lord, open my lips
and my mouth shall proclaim your praise.

(from Ps. 51)

To you Lord, I shall always stay near,
you hold me by your right hand;
you lead me by your counsel,
and will draw me in the wake of your glory.

Whom else do I have in heaven?
With you, I desire nothing on earth;
my heart and my flesh may dissolve
but God is for ever my portion, my rock.

It is good to draw close to God,
I have made the Lord my refuge,
and now I will tell of all your works.

(from Ps. 73)

The Magnificat (Song of Mary)

My soul sings praises to the Lord,
my spirit rejoices in God my Saviour,
for he has been mindful of his humble servant;
henceforth all generations will call me blessed.

The Almighty has done great things for me;
holy is his name.
His mercy stretches from age to age
upon those who revere him.

He has put forth his arm in strength
scattering the proud-hearted.
He has cast down the mighty from their thrones
and lifted up the lowly.

He has filled the hungry with good things,
he has sent the rich away empty-handed.

He has helped his servant Israel
ever remembering his love,
the love he promised to our fathers,
to Abraham and his children for ever.

The *Magnificat* and other biblical songs can be used like a psalm.

Bible readings

Choose one or two readings which are not too long and do not require explanation (more difficult passages can be left for other occasions, for example a Bible study group).

Here is a selection of a few key passages. To help identify each reading, its *name* (in italics) or else a sentence from it is given.

Genesis 12. 1–5	*The call of Abraham*
Gen. 50. 15–20	*Joseph forgives his brothers*
Leviticus 19. 33–34	*Love of strangers*
Deuteronomy 8. 2–3, 10–15	In riches, do not forget God.
1 Samuel 3. 1–10	*The Lord calls Samuel*
1 Kings 17. 8–16	*The widow of Zarephath*
1 Kings 19. 9–13a	*Elijah waits for the Lord on Mount Horeb*
Proverbs 3. 3–7	Trust in God, do not rely on your own understanding.
Prov. 4. 18–23	Keep watch over your heart: it is the wellspring of life.
Isaiah 11. 1–9	*Peace on earth*
Isa. 40. 27–31	Those who hope in the Lord will renew their strength.

Reading naturally, rather than with the declamatory style which is sometimes adopted, can help put the Word of God within our reach.

Remember to make sure that those whom you ask to read (both Bible readings and intercessions) will be heard clearly by everyone.

The *Letter from Taizé*, published every two months, gives a sentence of Scripture with a corresponding reference to a longer passage for every day of the year.

Isa. 42. 1–4,
   Isa. 49. 3–6 and
   Isa. 53. 1–5
	The Servant of the Lord

Isa. 43. 18–21	The Lord says: Do not dwell upon the past. See, I am doing something new!
Isa. 44. 21–23	The Lord says: I have swept away your sins like the morning mist.
Isa. 58. 5–11	If you do away with injustice, your night will become like the light of day.
Jeremiah 1. 4–8	*The Call of Jeremiah*
Jer. 29. 11–13	The Lord says: you will find me when you seek me with all your heart.
Jer. 31. 31–34	The Lord says: I will put my law deep within my people, I will write it on their hearts.
Ezekiel 36. 24–28	The Lord says: I will give you a new heart. I will put my Spirit in you.
Micah 6. 6,8	Act justly and walk humbly with your God.
Matthew 5. 1–12	*The Beatitudes*
Matt. 5. 13–16	*Salt and Light*
Matt. 6. 25–34	Do not worry about your life. Seek first the Kingdom and its righteousness.
Matt. 7. 7–11	Ask, and it will be given to you. Seek, and you will find.
Matt. 7. 21–27	*The house built on rock*
Matt. 11. 25–30	Jesus said: Come to me, for I am gentle and humble in heart, and you will find rest.
Matt. 13. 44–46	*The parables of the Pearl and the Treasure*

Matt. 16. 13–20	*Peter's profession of faith*
Matt. 16. 21–28	Jesus said: Anyone who loses their life for my sake will find it.
Matt. 20. 17–28 or Mark 9. 33–37	Whoever wants to be great among you must be your servant.
Matt. 21. 28–31	*The parable of the two sons*
Mark 1. 9–20	*The call of the first disciples*
Mark 2. 13–17	Jesus said: I have not come to call the righteous, but sinners.
Mark 4. 26–29	The Kingdom of God is like a seed that sprouts and grows, without us knowing how.
Mark 4. 35–41	*The calming of the storm*
Mark 6. 30–44 or John 6. 1–15	*The feeding of the five thousand*
Mark 10. 13–16	The Kingdom of God belongs tho those who are like children.
Mark 10. 17–30	*Leaving all to follow Jesus*
Mark 13. 33–37	Be alert, stay awake!
Mark 14. 3–9	*Jesus anointed at Bethany*
Luke 1. 26–45	*Mary learns of the birth of Jesus*
Luke 6. 27–38	Love your enemies. Do not judge.
Luke 9. 57–62	*The cost of following Jesus*
Luke 10. 25–37	*The good Samaritan*
Luke 10. 38–42	*Martha and Mary*
Luke 15. 11–32	*The Prodigal Son*
Luke 17. 20–21	The Kingdom of God is within you.
Luke 19. 1–10	*Zacchaeus*

Luke 23. 33–49	*The Crucifixion*
Luke 24. 1–8 or John 20. 1–10	*The Resurrection*
Luke 24. 13–35	*The Risen Christ on the road to Emmaus*
John 3. 1–8	*Nicodemus*
John 4. 1–15	*Jesus and the Samaritan woman*
John 6. 56–69	Lord, to whom shall we go? You have the words of eternal life.
John 10. 7–15	*The Good Shepherd*
John 11. 17–27	Jesus said: I am the Resurrection.
John 13. 1–15	*Jesus washes his disciples' feet*
John 14. 23–29	Do not let your hearts be troubled.
John 15. 1–8	Jesus said: I am the vine, you are the branches.
John 17. 15–23	*Jesus' prayer for his disciples*
John 20. 11–18	*Jesus appears to Mary Magdalene*
John 21. 15–19	*The Risen Christ with Peter*
Acts 2. 42–47 and Acts 4. 32–35	*The community of the first believers*
Romans 5. 1–11	God has shown his love for us in this: While we were still sinners, Christ died for us.
Rom. 8. 22–29	*God's Spirit prays in us*
Rom. 8. 31b–39	Nothing can separate us from the love of God in Christ.
Rom. 12. 1–5	In Christ, we who are many form one body.
Rom. 12. 9–16a	Bless those who persecute you.
1 Corinthians 12. 12–17, 27	*The Body of Christ*
1 Cor. 13	Love will never fail.

2 Cor. 4. 5–10	We bear the treasure of the Gospel in jars of clay to show it comes from God and not from us.
2. Cor. 4. 16–18	We fix our eyes not on what is seen, but on what is unseen.
2 Cor. 5. 16–20	God has entrusted to us the message of reconciliation.
Galatians 2. 20	I no longer live, but Christ lives in me.
Gal. 3. 26–4. 7	You are all sons of God, you are all one in Christ Jesus.
Ephesians 3. 14–19	May you know the love of Christ which surpasses all understanding.
Eph. 4. 1–6	Keep the unity of the Spirit through the bond of peace.
Philippians 2. 1–11	*Imitating Christ's humility*
Phil. 3. 7–14	Everything is a loss compared with the surpassing greatness of knowing Christ Jesus
Phil. 4. 4–7	Rejoice in the Lord! Do not be anxious about anything.
Colossians 1. 15–20	*Christ, the head of all creation*
Col. 3. 1–4	Set your hearts on things above.
Col. 3. 12–17	Forgive as the Lord forgave you.
1 Thess. 5. 14–24	Pray at all times, give thanks in all circumstances, for this is God's will for you in Christ.
Hebrews 4. 12–16	Jesus knows our weaknesses: he was tempted in every way as we are.
Heb. 12. 1–3	Let us throw off sin that so easily entangles, and fix our eyes on Jesus.

James 1. 12–18   God does not tempt anyone.

James 1. 22–25   Do not merely listen to the word of God: put it into practice

1 Peter 1. 3–9   Though you have not seen Christ, you love him.

1 Peter 4. 12–14   *Suffering with Christ*

2 Peter 3. 8–9, 13–14 *The patience of God*

1 John 3. 1–3   We are children of God!

1 John 3. 18–20   If our hearts condemn us, God is greater than our hearts.

1 John 4. 7–12   This is love: not that we loved God, but that he loved us and sent his Son for our forgiveness.

Revelation 22. 1–5   The servants of God will see his face.

Silence

After the reading(s), a chant can be sung to lead into a period of silent prayer.

Many of those who come to Taizé find important the long space of silence which there is during each of the common prayers. Words are often so inadequate to express our prayer and the prayer of Christ within us.

It is best to have just one longish (5–10 minute) period of silence during the prayer, rather than several. (Decide in advance who will indicate the end of the silence!)

Probably silence will be unusual for some of those who have come to the prayer you have prepared, so it is good to mention before the prayer begins that there will be a few minutes' complete silence.

Intercessions:
prayer for all humanity

This prayer can be introduced by singing *Kyrie Eleison*, an ancient response of the Church which means 'Lord, have mercy'. *Kyrie Eleison* (see page 41), or other suitable response, can be repeated after each intercession.

— May your peace shine among us, may your love set us free, Lord we pray.

— Enable us to be fervent in believing and constant in faith; set in our hearts a longing for your Kingdom, Lord we pray.

— That the leaders of the nations may seek the way that leads to peace, and that human rights may be everywhere respected, Lord we pray.

— Guide your Church in the way of the Gospel: may your Holy Spirit keep her faithful and warm-hearted, Lord we pray.

— Teach us to recognize your presence in every person, and above all in those who suffer, Lord we pray.

— For all who are homeless, for families searching for a place to live, and for refugees driven from their home, Lord we pray.

— For prisoners of conscience throughout the world, and especially for those who are tortured, Lord we pray.

— Teach those who have plenty to share the fruits of the earth among all mankind, Lord we pray.

— Let us pray for the elderly and the infirm, as their strength diminishes, increase their confidence in your love, Lord we pray.

— Watch over our families and all who are dear to us, Lord we pray.

— Let us pray for the visible unity of Christians: gather us together, Lord our God.

It is a good idea to ask several people, rather than just one, to read the intercessions. If you write some intercessions on slips of paper before the prayer, it is easy to ask people to read from their places.

— That we may be set free from our faults and set others free by our forgiveness, Lord we pray.

— Bring justice to our world, that all people may live in the joy of your peace, Lord we pray.

— That the Church may go out to meet all people, and become a place of trust and welcome, Lord we pray.

— Watch over those who are oppressed because of their race or religion: may their dignity be respected and their rights upheld, Lord we pray.

— For all who strive for justice: sustain their hope, Lord we pray.

— For the sick and all who care for them, Lord we pray.

— Let us pray for the dying, may God reveal to them the light of his presence.

— For us who are gathered here: may we spend our lives in the service of others, Lord we pray.

— Give us courage when things go wrong, strengthen us with faith in you, Lord we pray.

— Give us the spirit of prayer and praise, may we always and everywhere give you thanks, Lord we pray.

It is not necessary always to use the whole of one of these litanies, but after a few prepared intercessions time may be left for people to express intercessions in their own words, with everyone joining to sing *Kyrie Eleison* after each prayer.

— May our lives be filled with your compassion, give us a spirit of forgiveness and generosity of heart, Lord we pray.

— Give us a longing for the unity of the Church, may we rejoice in the gifts of others, Lord we pray.

— Give your Spirit to artists and musicians, may their work inspire us in our life with you, Lord we pray.

— For all who are beginning to know Christ, and who long to centre their lives on his will, Lord we pray.

— For those who cannot believe, and who give their lives in the service of others, Lord we pray.

— Give to married people the strength of your peace, and the grace to live together in love constantly renewed, Lord we pray.

— Support those who meet with difficulty and disappointment, renew their confidence and sense of purpose, Lord we pray.

— For the sick and for those who live in constant pain, Lord we pray.

— For those who have known the ravages of war and hatred, may they also know the peace you give, Lord we pray.

— For the work of pastors and church leaders, and for the ministry of each and every Christian, Lord we pray.

— Lead us by your Spirit to do your will; transform our hearts in accordance with your will, Lord we pray.

— Set us free from our sins, Lord, deliver us from our fears.

— For those who are sad, faced by difficulties or temptation, needing help and compassion, Lord we pray.

— Look upon your Church and direct her in the ways of unity, service and praise, Lord we pray.

— Be the salvation of our brothers and sisters who are oppressed, deliver those who are in prison for their faith, Lord we pray.

— We pray for all those who hurt or oppress us; forgive us for the times when we have hurt others, Lord we pray.

— For all who suffer from difficulties in their families, grant them your love which heals, Lord we pray.

— For those whose work is hard and unrewarding, and for those who can find no work, grant them the justice of your love. Lord, hear us we pray.

— For those who work for racial harmony and justice, and who create friendship between people of different cultures, Lord we pray.

— For Christians and for the believers of all religions, let us invoke the one and only God. Lord hear us we pray.

— For scientists and scholars, that their studies may serve the well-being of all mankind, let us ask the light of God.

— Keep us from despair and the fear of what is to come. May your love in us overcome all things, Lord we pray.

— For all Christians throughout the world, that each person may be a servant of Christ, truly and faithfully. Lord we pray.

— Renew your peace in our hearts, and give us the courage of faith in our daily life, Lord we pray.

— Free us from all prejudice and fear, deepen our understanding and our love, Lord we pray.

— May those in authority work to establish justice and freedom in their countries and throughout the world, Lord we pray.

— Show us the way to bring your compassion to the poor, the sick, the lonely and the unloved, Lord we pray.

— For all who are striving to follow in the steps of Christ, and for those who are longing for the gift of faith, Lord we pray.

— For those who seek to be bearers of friendship to young and old, across the age-barriers, Lord we pray.

— For all who are in prison, condemned, or exiled from their home, Lord we pray.

— For parents and teachers and all those entrusted with the care of children and young people, Lord we pray.

— Forgive those who oppress us or distort our best intentions; forgive us also and remedy our acts of injustice. Lord, hear us we pray.

— For all who, through addiction, have lost their health and freedom, give those who care for them patient understanding and a persevering love, Lord we pray.

— Console those who are bereaved or in sorrow, Lord we pray.

— God our Father, you care for us and know all our needs, may we find rest in your love.

— Lord, have mercy on us and heal our souls, for we have sinned against you.

— Renew the communion among Christians, healing their divisions, so that the world may believe in your love, Lord we pray.

— For justice and peace in our society, for the overcoming of barriers of fear, resentment and distrust, Lord we pray.

— For those who suffer want and anxiety through lack of work, Lord we pray.

— For those who are separated from their families, and those who have no home or family, Lord we pray.

— For the victims of drought and famine throughout the world, for the generous sharing of the world's resources, Lord we pray.

— For all who suffer trials and affliction and who need kindness and help, Lord we pray.

— Keep all who have found you rooted in your love; may they grow in goodness and truth, Lord we pray.

— Keep in your faithfulness, Lord, all who live in the mutual love of marriage. Renew in their commitment those who lead lives of celibacy for your Kingdom. Hear us we pray.

— We remember those who have died in the peace of Christ, and those whose faith is known only to you. Grant us to enter with them into the life that never ends, Lord we pray.

— Grant us, Lord, the joy of praise, in communion with all your saints.

Two Prayers of Adoration

O Jesus Christ, born in humility to raise up the humble,

— Adoramus te Domine.

You lived among us, healing the sick, proclaiming Good News to the poor and freedom to prisoners,

— Adoramus te Domine.

Jesus, you are kind and forgiving, you carry for us all that is more than we can bear,

— Adoramus te Domine.

Jesus, gentle and humble of heart, you call all who toil and are burdened,

— Adoramus te Domine.

You came to loose the chains of every captivity, friend of the poor, bread of hungry hearts,

— Adoramus te Domine.

You came into the world not to be served but to serve and give your life.

— Adoramus te Domine.

Jesus, by your resurrection from the dead you live for ever, to walk with us on the road to your Father and our Father,

— Adoramus te Domine.

— O Christ, in your resurrection you have destroyed sin and death.

— O Christ, in your resurrection you have brought all humanity from death to life.

— O Christ, in your resurrection you spoke joyful news to the women and the apostles, and salvation for the whole world.

— O Christ, in your resurrection you breathed the Holy Spirit upon your disciples.

— O Christ, in your resurrection you promised to be with us to the end of time.

— O Christ, in your resurrection you sent out your apostles to the ends of the earth.

— O Christ, in your resurrection you are the beginning, the Firstborn from among the dead.

— O Christ, in your resurrection you reconcile all things on earth and in heaven.

26

Prayers

The intercessions can be concluded by a song or by saying together the Lord's Prayer. Then a final prayer can be said, perhaps one of these prayers by Brother Roger.

O Christ,
tirelessly you seek out those who are looking for you
and who think that you are far away;
teach us, at every moment,
to place our spirits in your hands.
While we are still looking for you,
already you have found us.
However poor our prayer,
you hear us far more than we can imagine or believe.

Jesus, Risen Lord,
you change and transfigure our heart just as it is.
You do not even ask us to uproot the weeds;
you take care of that.
With our own wounds, the thorns that hurt us, you
light a fire — and a way forward opens in us to
welcome your Spirit of compassion and the Spirit of
praise that brings healing.
So that what is most resistant in us, our failures,
our refusals and our inner abysses, may be transfigured
into energies of love and reconciliation,
all you ask of us is that we welcome you
and rejoice in the miracle of your forgiveness.

Lord Christ,
at times we are like strangers on this earth,
disconcerted by all the violence and harsh
oppositions.
Like a gentle breeze,
You breathe upon us the Spirit of peace.
Transfigure the deserts of our doubts
and so prepare us to be bearers of reconciliation
wherever you place us,
until a hope of peace arises in our world.

Christ of compassion,
seeking to listen to you deep in our heart,
means knowing that you are always here,
that you understand everything.
And yet more:
you want to enable us to discern
a reality of the Kingdom of God,
something which cannot ever become worn out.

Christ Jesus,
you wish for us to be where you are.
And you give us what we scarcely dared hope for:
your unshakeable trust in us.
By your trust, you untie the knots
that hold us captive
and you make us more human.

Agreeing to lose everything for you, O Christ,
in order to take hold of you,
as you have already taken hold of us,
means abandoning ourselves to the living God.
Centring our life on you, Christ Jesus,
means daring to choose:
leaving ourselves behind so as to no longer walk
on two roads at the same time:
saying no to all that keeps us from following you,
and yes to all that brings us closer to you,
and through you, to those whom you entrust to us.

Close to you, Christ Jesus,
it becomes possible to know the realities of God,
by letting the little that we understand of the
Gospel pass into our daily life.
And this little proves to be just enough for us
to advance, day by day, moment by moment.
You never turn us into people who have made it,
but humble people of God who, in all simplicity,
are seeking to place their trust in you.

Lord Christ,
had we faith enough to move mountains,
without love
what would we be?
But you love us.
Without your Spirit who lives in our hearts,
what would we be?
But you love us.
Taking everything upon yourself,
you open for us a way towards the peace of God,
who wants neither suffering nor human distress.
Spirit of the Risen Christ.
Spirit of compassion, Spirit of praise,
your love for each one of us
will never fail.

Risen Jesus,
when we forget you, it is we who are absent.
But you remain present at all times,
deep within us.
Sometimes we start looking backwards,
and let ourselves be overrun by regret
or the nostalgia of the recent or distant past.
Holy Spirit, you who dwell in us always,
enable us to receive you
with a trusting heart, in faith,
so as to live quite simply in the present moment,
nothing more.

O Christ,
you take upon yourself all our burdens
so that freed of all that weighs us down,
we can constantly begin anew to walk
with lightened step,
from worry towards trusting,
from the shadows towards the clear flowing waters,
from our own will towards the vision of the coming
Kingdom.
And then we know,
though we had hardly dared hope it,
that you offer to make every human being
a reflection of your face.

Breath of the Spirit of God,
you place faith within each one of us,
faith which is such a simple trust in you
that it is possible for all to receive it.
Without us yet being able to see clearly,
you enlighten within, O Christ,
even in the opaque regions of our being.

Holy Spirit of God,
open in us the gates of simplicity
in order to dare to surrender ourselves to you
and to entrust everything to you in humble prayer.
Risen Christ, you could manage without us,
and yet you associate us so closely to God
that wherever there is a human being, God is present.

Breath of the love of God,
for whoever places their trust in you,
you uncover the wellspring
from which the unexpected flows.
Yet sometimes our prayer is so impoverished:
it is a sigh, a clumsy language.
But you understand all human expression.
In an inner life that has neither beginning nor end,
you allow us to rest in you, in body and spirit.

Following you, O Christ,
means passing time and time again
through the mystery of death and resurrection
— that Passover which remains incomprehensible
for our human condition.
Whenever we encounter you, you ask us to leave
ourselves behind and to follow you;
at those moments when,
if we are to love with you and not without you,
we must abandon some project contrary to your plan,
come Lord Christ,
so that we may realize that your love will never
disappear,
come and fill us with the quiet assurance that
to follow you is to give our life.

Spirit of the Risen Christ,
open us to this gospel reality:
being like salt which does not lose its savour.
This salt is a love without ulterior motives,
and nothing can then be lost in our lives,
unless it be by rejecting a spirit of mercy.
O Living God, you ask us nothing
but to welcome the gift of your love,
which you offer unconditionally,
without any strings attached.

Risen Christ,
today, tomorrow and always,
your Spirit lives in us.
Sometimes we feel we understand so little.
But remaining in your presence, wherever we are,
is prayer.
And perhaps close to you, O Christ,
silence is often everything in prayer.
And then we sense that, our whole life long,
we advance when trust in you guides every step,
when a trusting heart is at the beginning of everything.

You are the God of every human being
and, too bright for us to look upon,
you let yourself be seen as in a mirror,
on the face of your Christ.
We are eager to glimpse a reflection of your presence
in the confusion of people and events:
open in us the gateway to transparency of heart.
In that place of solitude
which there is in each one of us,
come and refresh the dry and thirsty ground
of our body and our spirit.
Come and inundate us with your trust
till even our inner deserts burst into flower.

Lord Christ,
For us who tell you: 'Lord, I believe, come and help
my lack of faith', you open a path of creation.
And on this path, you enable us to create even with
our own frailty.
Praised be the Risen Christ, who, knowing us to be
poor and vulnerable, comes to pray within us the hymn
of an unchanging confidence.

Risen Jesus,
you are there close beside each person,
you descend to where we are,
to the very lowest point of our human condition.
And you take upon yourself all that hurts us,
both in ourselves and in others.
You accompany every human being.
More than that,
you visit even those who, as non-believers, have
died without having been able to know you.
And so, in our inner struggle,
the contemplation of your forgiveness
gives rise to a radiant goodness
in the humble heart that allows itself to be led
by your Spirit.

Lord Christ, you take us
with our hearts just as they are.
Why should we wait for our hearts to be changed,
in order to go to you?
You change them, day by day,
without our knowing how.
You have all that is needed to heal us:
prayer, hymns, forgiveness,
and the springtime of reconciliations.

Praised be the living God
for the multitude of women, men and children
who throughout the world
are searching, striving, and giving their lives
in order to be bearers of reconciliation.
Through the repentance of our hearts,
and the spirit of simplicity of the beatitudes,
you clothe us with forgiveness, as with a garment.
Enable us to welcome the realities of the Gospel
with a childlike heart,
and to discover your will,
which is love and nothing else.

Christ Jesus, by your Spirit
you come and kindle a burning light in us.
We know well that it is not we
who create this source of light,
but you the Risen Lord.
To all of us, you give the one thing that matters
and which is hidden from our own eyes:
a peaceful trust in God
and also poverty in spirit,
so that with a great thirst for the realities of God,
we may take the risk of letting you accompany us
O Christ,
and of accompanying, in our turn,
those whom you entrust to us.

O living God,
you no longer knew how to express to human beings
that you are nothing but love and forgiveness,
that you never want suffering for anyone on the
earth, that you never punish.
And so, to make yourself understood,
you came on the earth in poverty,
through your Christ.
Now risen from the dead, Christ Jesus is present
by his Spirit in every person,
he is there for those who suffer trials.
As we advance with you, one day we shall tell you:
sing in me O Christ,
your love has burnt into my soul.

Lord Christ, enable us to place our trust in you,
and so to live in the present moment.
So often we forget that you never want human
suffering, but peace in our hearts.
Christ Jesus, by your Spirit you dwell in us.
More still, you pray in us.
Your miracle within us is accomplished
through the trust we have in you
and your continual forgiveness.

O Christ, you do not make of our lives,
nor of your Church, a place of monotony.
For you give each human being such different gifts;
and for every person to become who they are
in their heart of hearts, a song arises in them
to the point that difficulties can stimulate faith to
build even with the hard events of life.
In this way, O Christ, you offer an inner springtime,
and right to the bottom of the darkness in our hearts
your song is present, piercing our night:
darkness is no darkness before you,
the night is as light as the day.

O living God,
in our darkness you kindle a fire that never dies out.
Through the spirit of praise, you take us out of ourselves.
To us, the poor of God, you have entrusted a mystery of hope.
In our human frailty,
you have set a spiritual strength that is never withdrawn.
Even when we are unaware of it, it is always there,
ready to carry us onward.
Yes, in our darkness, you kindle a fire that never dies out.

In following you, O Christ,
we choose to love and not to harden our hearts,
even when the incomprehensible happens.
As we remain in your presence with perseverance,
day after day, and pray with simplicity of heart,
you come and make us into people
who are a leaven of confident trust by the way we live.
And all that your Gospel calls us to,
all that you ask of us, you give.

A Prayer around the Cross

Christians have always celebrated week by week the central mystery of their faith: the mystery of Easter (the Paschal mystery), the passing-over from death to life accomplished by Christ. The mystery of the death and resurrection of Christ illuminates the mystery of our own lives, we who are continually passing from doubt and anxiety to confident trust, and through 'little deaths' to new life.

Several years ago, some Christians in Eastern Europe suggested that we have a prayer around the cross at Taizé in the same way that they do. At the end of the evening prayer on Friday, the icon cross is laid down flat in the centre of the church, supported on a couple of low cushions or stools. While the singing continues, those who wish come close to the cross to pray.

Another way in which Christians, from the earliest times, have celebrated the Paschal mystery is by singing the joy of the resurrection in a vigil of prayer in the dark of night.

On entering the darkened church everyone is given a small candle. During the singing of a church is lit up. The story of the resurrection or other passage of the Gospel can be read

before the vigil continues.

If people are to gather on two successive evenings to pray then there could be a prayer around the cross on the first evening (Friday) and a celebration of the resurrection and the light of Christ on the next evening.

Many parishes and groups throughout the world have since taken up this suggestion from Eastern Europe — either for a regular weekly or monthly prayer, or else for occasional prayer vigils.

To kneel close to the cross and perhaps place our foreheads for a moment on it is a gesture which signifies our desire to entrust everything to Christ. It is a way, other than in words, of expressing our prayer. The cross reminds us that Christ knows what it is to be human, and that now, risen from the dead, he accompanies every human being in his or her suffering, even when his presence is not recognized.

A prayer around the cross can be sustained by the singing of meditative chants, perhaps interspersed with periods of silence, or the reading of a prayer.

Can some of these ideas be used for our Sunday morning worship?

Rather than having a very definite start and finish, could the service or mass begin by people gathering in prayer — in silence with music, or singing a simple chant? And at the end, could the prayer be prolonged in a similar way?

Could a meditative chant and period of silence be introduced into our Sunday morning service? (For example, a chant which is sung after the Gospel or sermon, or else during the communion, can lead in naturally to a time of silence.)

Can an area at the front of the church be covered with mats or carpet, so that children and young people who want to can kneel to pray there? Many love the simplicity of kneeling on the floor, which is both informal and a gesture of prayer.

Arranging the church or room for prayer

When possible pray in a church. Praying in a place where Christians of the neighbourhood gather every Sunday can be one visible sign of our prayer being united to that of the whole Church.

Prepare in simple beauty: take away superfluous objects from the sanctuary area; use a cross, an icon or an open Bible, and with candles and maybe flowers and fabric, make the area towards which people are seated as prayerful as possible.

Arrange some mats or carpet for those who wish to kneel or sit, and benches or chairs behind or round the side.

To pray facing the same way, towards the cross or altar, rather than sitting in a closed circle, can remind us that in our prayer together we are seeking Christ: our prayer is not centred on ourselves.

Discreet lighting, which is not too bright, helps us not to be self-conscious, and is restful for the eyes. (One can always turn on more lights just for hymns etc. if necessary.)

SONGS
AND
CHANTS

Going over the songs together before the prayer, can be already like the beginning of the prayer. The person teaching the songs should see it as a pastoral service rather than 'conducting'. He or she should not conduct during the prayer itself. The aim is not musical perfection, but simply to find a way of expressing our prayer in the beauty of song.

Even if time is limited, it is good to sing through both the melody line (soprano part) and also the lowest line of harmony (bass part), for even if only a small number of people are able to sing the bass or other parts it will straightaway make a great difference. Singing the harmony lines one by one, or else playing them on the piano, can help people learn very quickly.

A very effective way of singing the canons (rounds) is for the male voices to start all together and then for the female voices to join in in canon, or vice-versa.

When teaching the songs and leading them, be attentive to the rhythm, making sure that they do not drag and thereby become sad.

1. Alleluia 2

Alleluia is a Hebrew word meaning *Praise the Lord*

(Solo: Al - le - lu - ia)

Al - le - lu - - -

- ia, al - le - lu - - - ia____

2. Alleluia 4

(Solo: Al - le - lu - ia)

Al - le - lu -

- ia al - le - lu - ia al - le - lu - ia ____

3. Alleluia 7

Al - le - lu - ia, al - le - lu - ia, al - le -

- lu - - ia! Al - le - lu - ia, al - le -

- lu - ia, al - le - lu - - ia!

40

4. Kyrie 1 Kyrie Eleison are Greek words meaning *Lord, have mercy*

Ky-ri-e, Ky-ri-e, e-le-i-son

5. Kyrie 6

Ky-ri-e e-le-i-son, Ky-ri-

-e e-le-i-son

6. Kyrie 10

Ky-ri-e, Ky-ri-e, e-le-i-son;

Ky-ri-e, Ky-ri-e, e-le-i-son

If the intercessions are *sung* all may hold the last note of the *Kyrie eleison*, humming it as a background, while the soloist improvises a tune. The hum changes to the final chord as the soloist sings 'Lord hear us we pray', or other ending, to the notes shown in brackets.

7. Adoramus te Domine

A-do-ra-mus te Do-mi - ne

We adore you, Lord.

8. The Beatitudes (Russian Orthodox melody)

1 - Happy all, who are poor in spir - it : for the King - dom of heaven is theirs
2 - Happy all those who now are weep - ing : the joy of God will com - fort them.
3 - Happy all the hum - ble, the gen - tle : for the earth one day will be theirs
4 - Happy all, who for just - ice hun - ger : they shall re - ceive their heart's de - sire.
5 - Happy all, who for - give - ness of - fer : for they shall al - so be for - given.
6 - Happy all with hearts clear and sim - ple : for they shall come to see their God.
7 - Happy all cre - a - tors of true peace : they shall be called the sons of God.
8 - Happy all suff' ring per - se - cu - tion: for the King - dom of heaven is theirs
9 - Happy all, who per - se - vere for Christ ; for in God they'll be filled with joy.

9. Benedictus Canon ①–②

Be – ne-di-ctus qui ve – nit,

Be – ne-di-ctus qui ve – nit, in

no – mi-ne, in no – mi-ne,

in no-mi-ne Do – mi-ni.

Blessed is the one who comes in the name of the Lord.

10. Bless the Lord (Psalm 103)

Bless the Lord my soul and

bless his ho-ly name.   Bless the Lord my

soul,   He res-cues me from death.

11. Confitemini Domino (Psalm 118)

Give thanks to the Lord for he is good.

12. Dona nobis pacem (Anon)

Do - na   no - bis   pa - cem, pa-cem;

do — na   no — bis   pa — — cem.

Do — — na   no — bis   pa - cem,

do - na   no - bis   pa — — cem.

Do — na   no — bis   pa - cem,

do - na   no - bis   pa — — cem.

Grant us peace.

13. Gloria Canon ①–②

(rhythmically)

Glo-ri-a, glo-ri-a, in ex-cel-sis De-o.

Glo-ri-a, glo-ri-a, al-le-lu-ia!

legato ②

et in ter-ra pax ho — mi – ni – bus

bo-nae vo-lun – ta – tis

Glory to God in the highest and on earth peace to men of good will.

14. Gloria Patri

Glo-ri-a, glo-ri-a, glo-ri-a

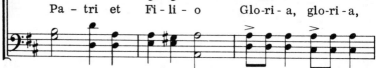

Pa – tri et Fi – li – o   Glo-ri-a, glo-ri-a,

glo-ri-a   Spi – ri – tu – i   Sanc – to

Glory to the Father, the Son, and the Holy Spirit.

15. In our darkness (Psalm 139)

In our dark – ness there is no dark-ness with you O Lord, the deep-est night is clear as the day _____ . In our

16. Jubilate Deo Canon ①–② (Praetorius)

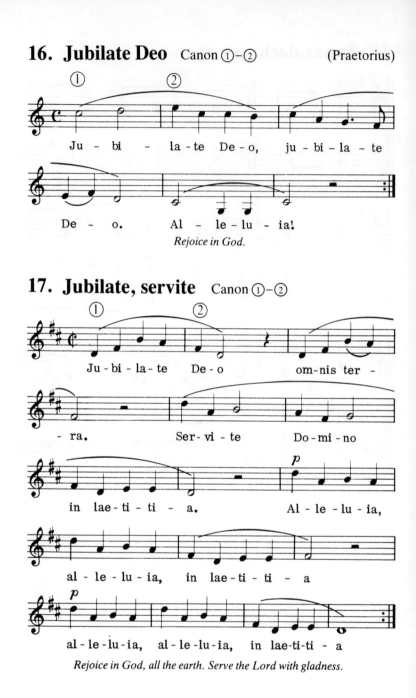

Ju – bi – la - te De - o, ju - bi – la – te

De – o. Al – le – lu – ia!

Rejoice in God.

17. Jubilate, servite Canon ①–②

Ju - bi - la - te De - o   om-nis ter -

- ra.   Ser- vi - te   Do - mi - no

in lae - ti - ti - a.   Al - le - lu - ia,

al - le - lu - ia,   in lae - ti - ti - a

al - le - lu - ia,   al - le - lu - ia,   in lae - ti - ti - a

Rejoice in God, all the earth. Serve the Lord with gladness.

18. Laudate omnes gentes

Lau — da — te om-nes gen-tes, lau-

— da — te Do-mi — num. Lau — da — te om-nes

(Fine)

gen-tes, lau — da — te Do-mi — num! Lau —

All peoples, praise the Lord.

19. Magnificat Canon ①–②

Ma – gni – fi – cat   Ma – gni – fi – cat

Ma – gni-fi-cat a – ni-ma me – a   Do-mi-num

Ma – gni-fi – cat   Ma – gni-fi – cat

Ma – gni-fi-cat a – ni – ma me – a

My soul magnifies the Lord.

20. My soul is at rest (Psalm 62)

My soul is at rest__ in God a - lone,
my sal-va - tion comes from him. My

Fine

21. O Lord, hear my prayer (Psalm 102)

O Lord hear my prayer, O Lord hear my prayer.

When I call an – swer me. O

Lord hear my prayer, O Lord hear my prayer

Fine

Come and lis-ten to me. O

22. Ostende nobis Canon ①–②

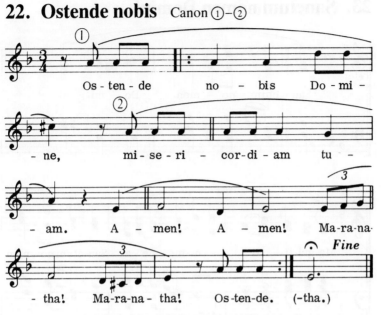

Os - ten - de   no – bis   Do - mi –
– ne,   mi - se - ri – cor-di - am   tu –
– am.   A – men!   A – men!   Ma-ra-na-
– tha!   Ma-ra-na - tha!   Os -ten-de.   (-tha.)

Lord, show us your mercy. Amen! Come soon!

23. Sanctum nomen Domini

My soul magnifies the holy name of the Lord.

24. Stay with us (Luke 24)

Stay with us O Lord Je-sus Christ:
night will soon fall. Then stay with us O
Lord Je-sus Christ: light in our dark-ness.

25. Surrexit Canon ①–②

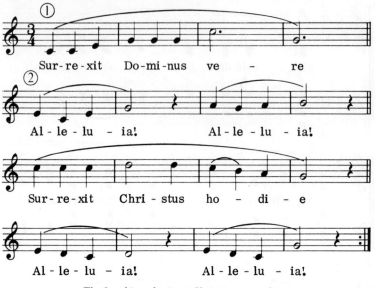

Sur-re-xit Do-mi-nus ve – re

Al - le - lu – ia! Al - le - lu – ia!

Sur-re-xit Chri - stus ho – di - e

Al - le - lu – ia! Al - le - lu – ia!

The Lord is truly risen. Christ is risen today.

26. Tallis' Canon

Thomas Tallis c.1505–85

Praise God, from whom all bless-ings flow,

Praise Him, all crea-tures here be - low,

Praise Him a - bove, ye heaven-ly host,

Praise Fa - ther, Son, and Ho - ly Ghost.

27. The Lord is my light (Psalm 27)

Theme I

The Lord is my light, my light and sal-va-tion; in him I trust, in · him I trust. The

Theme II

The Lord is my light, my light and sal-va-tion: in him I trust, in him I trust. The

Each of the two themes can be sung *separately* either in unison or as a round (two voices only: coming in on A and B). The two themes can be sung *together*, preferably with theme I for female voices and theme II for male voices.

28. Ubi caritas

U – bi ca – ri – tas et
a – – mor U – bi ca – ri –
– tas De-us i – bi est

Where there is love and charity, there is God.

29. Veni Creator Spiritus Canon ①–②

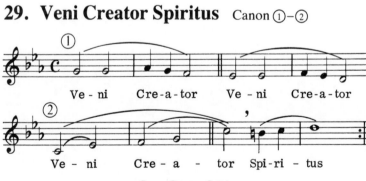

Ve - ni Cre -a-tor Ve - ni Cre -a-tor
Ve - ni Cre - a - tor Spi -ri - tus

Come Creator Spirit.

More Words and Music

Music from Taizé, Vol. I and Vol. II: these 2 volumes contain nearly all the songs in this book and many more. They include solo parts to be sung over the chants and music for guitar or keyboard accompaniment (an Instrumental Edition for each volume, for accompaniment by other instruments is also available). (*Collins Liturgical Publications*)

More of Brother Roger's reflections and prayers are contained in *Parable of Community,* and in his journal (6 paperback volumes). (*Mowbray*)

Cassettes

Canons et Litanies / Cantate / Resurrexit / Alleluia!
(Also *Chanter Ensemble:* a learning aid)

All the above are available from Mowbrays' main bookshop:
28 Margaret St, London W1N 7LB (Tel: 01-580-2812), and other Christian booksellers.

The *Letter from Taizé* is published bi-monthly by the community in 9 languages. It contains reflections on biblical themes and gives news of the experiences of those striving for reconciliation in every part of the world. For each day it gives a short Bible reading which is the same as the one read at Taizé at the midday prayer. An annual subscription costs: £4.00 (UK), IR £4.50 (Ireland), $6.00 (USA), 40 Skr (Sweden), $12.00 (Australia), $15.00 (N.Z.), $10.00 (Canada). Correspondence: 'Letter from Taizé', Taizé Community, 71250 CLUNY, France.

FOR INFORMATION ABOUT THE MEETINGS AT TAIZÉ, write to:

Taizé Community,   Tel: France 85.50.18.18 (Meetings information)
71250 CLUNY,   85.50.14.14 (Community)
France   Telex: COTAIZE 800753

Reprinted 1989

ISBN 0 264 67167 8

Printed in Great Britain by Hollen Street Press Ltd., Slough, Berkshire.